12/13

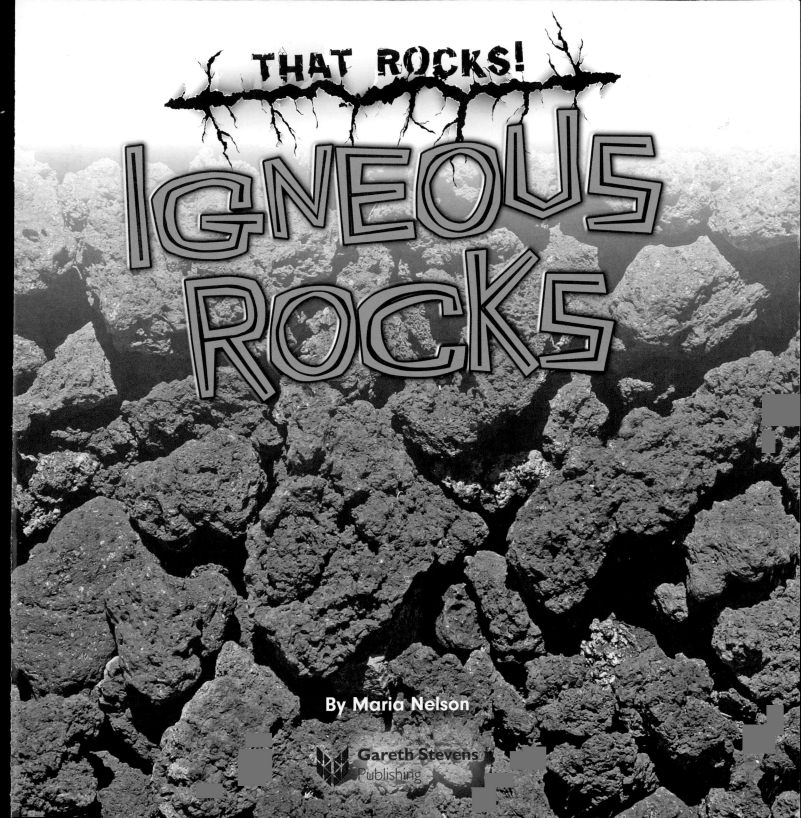

# THAT ROCKS!

# IGNEOUS ROCKS

By Maria Nelson

**Gareth Stevens**
Publishing

Please visit our website, www.garethstevens.com. For a free color catalog of all our high-quality books, call toll free 1-800-542-2595 or fax 1-877-542-2596.

**Library of Congress Cataloging-in-Publication Data**

Library of Congress Cataloging-in-Publication Data

Nelson, Maria.
Igneous rocks / Maria Nelson.
    pages cm. -- (That rocks!)
Includes bibliographical references and index.
ISBN 978-1-4339-8314-6 (pbk.)
ISBN 978-1-4339-8315-3 (6-pack)
ISBN 978-1-4339-8313-9 (library binding)
1.  Igneous rocks—Juvenile literature.  I. Title.
QE461.N433 2014
552'.1—dc23

2012047097

First Edition

Published in 2014 by
**Gareth Stevens Publishing**
111 East 14th Street, Suite 349
New York, NY 10003

Copyright © 2014 Gareth Stevens Publishing

Designer: Katelyn Londino
Editor: Kristen Rajczak

Photo credits: Cover, p. 1 John Orsbun/Shutterstock.com; p. 5 SAM YEH/AFP/Getty Images; p. 7 Pack-Shot/Shutterstock.com; p. 9 Visuals Unlimited, Inc./Gerald & Buff Corsi/Getty Images; p. 11 AFP/Getty Images; p. 13 Michael Zysman/Shutterstock.com; p. 14 (inset) Photo Researchers/Getty Images; p. 15 Nigel Halliwell/Oxford Scientific/Getty Images; p. 16 (inset) Tyler Boyes/Shutterstock.com; p. 17 BIOPHOTO ASSOCIATES/Photo Researchers/Getty Images; p. 18 (inset) Jasmin Awad/Photodisc/Getty Images; p. 19 Chris Rodenberg Photography/Shutterstock.com; p. 20 (inset) ollirg/Shutterstock.com.

Printed in the United States of America

CPSIA compliance information: Batch #CS13GS: For further information contact Gareth Stevens, New York, New York at 1-800-542-2595.

# CONTENTS

Words in the glossary appear in **bold** type the first time they are used in the text.

# A FIERY START

Deep within Earth, it's very hot. It can be 1,100 to 2,400°F (600 to 1,300°C)! That's hot enough to melt rock.

Our planet is largely made of rock that was once **molten** many miles underground. Some people call this "fire rock," but its scientific name is igneous rock. From black and glossy to white and holey, igneous rock can appear in many different forms. But it always starts out superhot beneath Earth's surface!

## SET IN STONE

The two other main kinds of rock are sedimentary rock and metamorphic rock.

Many landforms around the world are made of igneous rock.

# A COOL MOVE

Igneous rock forms when molten rock cools as it moves toward Earth's surface. While molten rock is underground, it's called magma. Magma rises because it has less **density** than the solid rocks around it.

One kind of igneous rock—intrusive igneous rock—forms when magma cools while it's still underground. It can form when magma is trapped in little pockets or tunnels deep within Earth or as magma moves to lower temperatures closer to Earth's surface. The magma that forms intrusive igneous rock cools slowly.

## SET IN STONE

The word "igneous" comes from the Latin word for "fire."

Even though it forms underground,
some intrusive igneous rock is later uncovered.

# MADE OF MINERALS

Igneous rock is made up of **minerals**. The slow, complete cooling of magma that forms intrusive igneous rocks lets some of these minerals "grow." This means they form the visible crystals that help scientists figure out which mineral they are.

Intrusive igneous rocks can be small and look somewhat like thick plant roots. They can also be huge **domes** and cover more than 40 square miles (104 sq km)! The **core** of mountain ranges may be made of intrusive igneous rocks, too.

## SET IN STONE

Intrusive igneous rock is sometimes called plutonic rock.

When you break open some intrusive igneous rocks,
you find a beautiful surprise!

# VOLCANOES

Another kind of igneous rock is extrusive. It forms when magma reaches Earth's surface and cools. One of the most common ways for this to happen is a volcanic **eruption**.

Once magma reaches Earth's surface, it's called lava. The mountainous landform that forms from the buildup of lava is what often comes to mind when you hear the word "volcano." However, a volcano is any **vent** in Earth's crust through which melted rock and hot gases escape.

## SET IN STONE

Many islands, such as those that make up the state of Hawaii, formed from volcanoes erupting. That means they're made of igneous rock!

The rock that makes up volcanoes like this one is extrusive igneous rock.

# OUTSIDE THE VOLCANO

Extrusive igneous rock forms in sheets as lava spreads over the ground and cools. It also forms from pieces of magma that shoot out the top of the volcano. That means you might find igneous rock miles from where a volcano erupted!

Extrusive igneous rock is made up of the same magma that intrusive igneous rock is. But since extrusive igneous rock cools so quickly, the minerals that may be in it don't have time to form crystals.

## SET IN STONE

One kind of extrusive igneous rock is called volcanic glass.

The sheets of igneous rock that cover the ground around a volcano are often called lava fields.

# INSIDE THE ROCKS

Scientists **identify** different kinds of igneous rock based on the minerals in them. One way to group igneous rocks is by how much of the mineral silica they contain. The igneous rocks with the most silica in them—66 percent or more—are called felsic. Igneous rocks that are less than 45 percent silica are called ultramafic.

Scientists use special tools to study a rock's **chemical** makeup. However, you can learn a lot about what's in an igneous rock just by looking at it.

## SET IN STONE

A volcanologist is a scientist who studies volcano formation and history. A geologist studies the matter that makes up Earth. They both might study igneous rocks!

Granite, shown here, is felsic.

# COLOR AND TEXTURE

The color of an igneous rock often shows what minerals make up the rock. For example, igneous rocks with a felsic **composition** are commonly light colors such as white, pink, or gray. Ultramafic rocks have darker colors like black or brown. Looking at a rock's color is one way to narrow down what kind of igneous rock it may be.

Texture can aid in igneous rock identification, too. When talking about igneous rocks, texture means the size of the crystals in the rocks.

obsidian

## SET IN STONE

An igneous rock's color doesn't tell its composition in every case. Obsidian is felsic—but it's a black or dark brown volcanic glass.

Igneous rocks may have a fine-grained texture, or have crystals that are too small to see without magnification. The rock pictured here has a coarse-grained texture, or large crystals that can be easily seen.

# COMMON IGNEOUS ROCK

You may have heard of one well-known kind of igneous rock—granite. Granite is light colored, showing that it's felsic. It's plutonic and has a coarse-grained texture. Granite was used for building in the past. Today, it's more common as the outer covering of buildings, kitchen countertops, and street curbs.

Basalt is another common igneous rock. It's an extrusive igneous rock that's commonly black. Basalt may appear very smooth or have a spongy look.

basalt necklace

## SET IN STONE

Granite is the most common type of rock making up the continents.

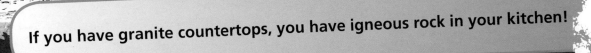

If you have granite countertops, you have igneous rock in your kitchen!

19

# FIND THEM WORLDWIDE

Igneous rocks can be some of the oldest rocks in the world. Studying them can teach us about the conditions of our planet millions of years ago. They might even contain clues about the first life on Earth!

Would you like to find an igneous rock? Anywhere a volcano has erupted in the past is a good place to start! From the smoking vents of Mount Etna in Italy to the ocean floor, these amazing rocks can be found all over the world.

Mount Etna

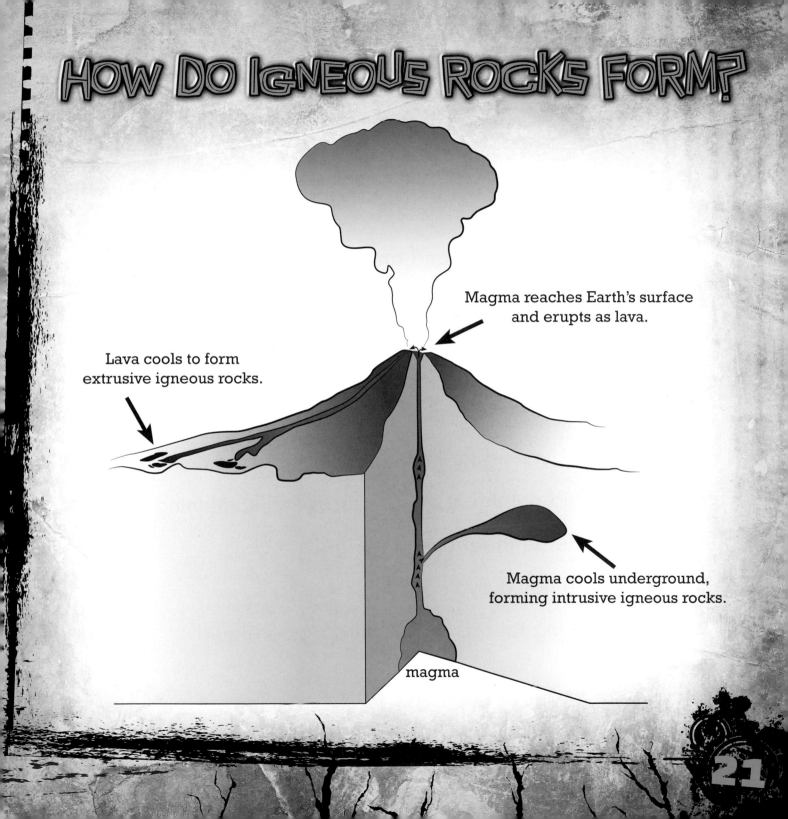

# HOW DO IGNEOUS ROCKS FORM?

Magma reaches Earth's surface and erupts as lava.

Lava cools to form extrusive igneous rocks.

Magma cools underground, forming intrusive igneous rocks.

magma

# GLOSSARY

**chemical:** relating to matter that can be mixed with other matter to cause changes

**composition:** the matter and arrangement of matter that makes up something

**core:** the central part of something

**density:** the amount of matter in a given area

**dome:** a rounded shape that looks like half a ball

**eruption:** the bursting forth of hot, liquid rock from within the earth

**identify:** to find out the name or features of something

**mineral:** matter in the ground that forms rocks

**molten:** made liquid by heat

**vent:** an opening for the escape of a gas or liquid

# FOR MORE INFORMATION

## Books

Hyde, Natalie. *What Is the Rock Cycle?* New York, NY: Crabtree Publishing, 2011.

Stille, Darlene R. *Igneous Rocks: From Fire to Stone*. Minneapolis, MN: Compass Point Books, 2008.

## Websites

**Cycles: The Rock Cycle**
*www.cotf.edu/ete/modules/msese/earthsysflr/rock.html*
Read about how rock forms, and see an illustration of the rock cycle.

**Igneous Rocks**
*geology.com/rocks/igneous-rocks.shtml*
Look at pictures of all kinds of igneous rocks.

# INDEX